D0476677

MuCountry

ina

Jillian Powell

W
FRANKLIN WATTS

This edition 2013

First published in 2012
by Franklin Watts
Copyright © Franklin Watts 2012

Franklin Watts
338 Euston Road
London NW1 3BH

Franklin Watts Australia
Level 17/207 Kent Street
Sydney, NSW 2000

Dewey number: 951'.0612
ISBN: 978 1 4451 2699 9
Library ebook: 978 1 4451 2425 4

Printed in Malaysia

Series Editor: Paul Rockett
Series Designer: Paul Cherrill
  for Basement68
Picture Researcher: Diana Morris

Franklin Watts is a division of
Hachette Children's Books,
an Hachette UK company.

www.hachette.co.uk

 Contents

All words in **bold**
appear in the
glossary on page 23.

 # China in the world

My name is Li and I come from China.

This is the **Chinese character** for my name:

力

In China we use characters instead of an alphabet.

Beijing

Shanghai

Hong Kong

China's place in the world.

Beijing is the capital city of China.

China is the fourth largest country in the world and the largest within Asia. It shares borders with fourteen other countries.

I live in Beijing. It is a big, busy city with tall skyscraper buildings and lots of amazing things to see.

People who live in China

More people live in China than any other country in the world. Most of us speak Mandarin Chinese but many other languages are spoken in different **regions**.

In the cities, people work in banks, shops, offices and factories.

6

Here are people working on a rice plantation in the countryside.

People live in cities or in small towns or villages in the countryside where they grow crops or herd sheep or goats.

We make clothes, toys, games and many other things that are sold all over the world.

China's landscape

China is so big it has many different types of landscape, from tall mountains and highlands to wide **deserts** and flat plains.

There are rivers and waterfalls, thick forests and rocky landforms of towers and caves.

Two-humped camels live in the Gobi Desert.

These people, dressed in traditional clothes, are picking tea leaves.

China has a long coastline and many islands. To the south-west are the Himalayan mountains.

Crops like tea grow on **terraces** cut into steep hillsides.

9

The weather in China

Winters are coldest in the north-east, where you can go skiing.

The weather is different all around China. In my city, Beijing, we have hot, rainy summers and cold, dry winters.

Summers are hottest in the south, between April and September, which is also the rainy season.

Much of the country has dry seasons and wet **monsoon** rains. The rain blows in from the Pacific Ocean and the Indian Ocean.

The monsoon begins in the south in springtime and reaches the north by July and August.

Beijing during the monsoon.

At home with my family

In China, most families who live in a city have only one child. I live with my mum and dad and my grandma.

We live in a flat which has three bedrooms, a bathroom and a cooking and dining area. There is also a small balcony.

our block of flats. We live on the ninth floor, so we can see over the city.

At the weekend we often go to the park together. Lots of people go there to have fun and exercise.

Sometimes Dad takes me go-karting with my friends. I also like shopping at the market with Grandma.

Street markets sell clothes and craftwork as well as foods.

My favourite pastimes are go-karting and ping pong. What are yours?

What we eat

we eat using spoons and chopsticks.

For breakfast, we have rice or noodles and drink tea. I have a hot lunch at school.

For dinner, we share dishes of meat, fish or **tofu**, rice and vegetables.

A kebab stall in Beijing. Kebabs are made of meat, seafoods and sometimes bugs like scorpions!

Kebabs and dim sum, which are little steamed dumplings or rolls with tasty fillings, are also popular in China.

They are eaten with tea in restaurants and sold by street sellers as fast food snacks.

My favourite food is dim sum!

 # Going to school

Most children start school when they are six years old.

Every morning we sing our **national anthem** and raise the Chinese flag.

We have lessons in Chinese language and literature, maths, and moral education which teaches us how to behave well towards others.

We salute the flag during the morning flag-raising ceremony.

In morning break, we do our exercises, which include lots of stretching.

At lunchtime, we listen to a story or we do some homework.

In the afternoons, we usually do sport or art and crafts.

Art lessons are fun! My favourite colour is red, which is a lucky colour in china.

Festivals and celebrations

We have lots of colourful festivals with fireworks and street parades.

Chinese New Year begins with the first new moon of the year. On the fifteenth day, there is a Lantern Festival.

For the Lantern Festival, children parade the streets carrying lanterns.

In spring, there is a Dragon Boat Festival when people race boats and eat special rice dumplings.

For children in China, our sixth birthday is an important one. Families get together and eat long noodles to bring us luck and a long life.

In dragon boat racing, the boat is decorated with a dragon's head.

I like Chinese New Year. Children are given red envelopes of money.

Things to see

Many people come to see the Great Wall of China, which is over 2,000 years old and runs for over 8,500km. It crosses mountains, deserts and plains. You can see part of the wall in my city, Beijing.

The Great Wall of China is the worlds longest wall.

Tourists like to see China's beautiful **pagodas**, and the famous **terracotta** soldiers and horses. This army was made for the **tomb** of the First Emperor of all China.

The Terracotta Army has over 8,000 soldiers and 600 horses, all life-size.

I want to go to see the giant pandas at the Chengdu Panda Base.

Here are some facts about my country!

Fast facts about China

Capital city = Beijing
Population = 1.35 billion
Currency = Yuan
Area = 9.6 million km^2
Main language = Mandarin Chinese
National holiday = Chinese New Year
Main religions = Buddhism, Islam,
   Christianity, Taoism
Longest river = Yangtze (6,300km)
Highest mountain = Mount Everest (8,848m)

Glossary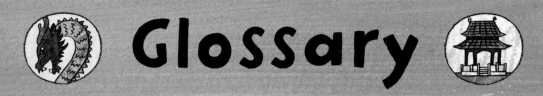

Chinese character a word written in the Chinese language

deserts dry lands which have little or no rain

monsoon heavy seasonal rains

national anthem a song of praise and love for a country

pagodas temples, often built as pyramids or towers

regions parts, or areas of a country

terraces flat areas, sometimes forming several levels

terracotta a type of red clay

tofu a soft, cheese-like food made from soya bean milk

tomb building that marks a grave

Websites

www.activityvillage.co.uk/china_for_kids.htm
Facts on China's people, history and culture, with puzzles, activities and crafts.

www.enchantedlearning.com/asia/china
Lots of facts and information, with special features and activities.

http://news.bbc.co.uk/cbbcnews/hi/specials/2005/china/
A report with diaries and blogs from children living in China.

Books

Been There: China by Annabel Savery (Franklin Watts, 2011)

Popcorn Countries: China by Alice Harman (Wayland, 2013)

Chinese New Year by Nancy Dickman (Heinemann Library, 2011)

Index